i

LIFE WITH BIRDIE

The African Grey Parrot

(Psittacus erithacus)

Helen L. Shevel

Baird Farms Publishing Company LLC, Mt. Juliet, TN 37122

This book is dedicated to my husband of 56 years, Glen Shevel.

H.

Copyright©2020 by Helen L. Shevel

No part of this book may be copied or downloaded, except for review or promotional purposes, without the written permission by the Publisher or Author.

Published in the United States of America.

First Edition

10 9 8 7 6 5 4 3 2 1

ISBN 978-1-945450-11-2

Baird Farms Publishing Company LLC.

Mount Juliet, TN 37122 wdjaq@aol.com

How does this story begin? When did it begin and why is it so fresh in my mind? How could a precious little African Grey Parrot, hatched on November 24, 1983, in Titusville, Florida, come to be the most wonderful little feathered friend to me? When you read this story, you will clearly understand it all.

Helen

Table of Contents

Forward	1
Romeo	3
Bird	5
Going Home	8
Back in Ohio	9
Red Tail Feathers	12
Learning to Speak	14
Merry Christmas	16
The Farm in Greenford	17
The Great Escape	19
Sweet Memories	22
Here We Go A-Traveling	23
Off to Alaska	25
Bird's Talents	28
Leaving the Farm	29
An Egg?	30
Birdie	32
Bed Time	33
Another Egg?	34
The Old Birdie	35
Clipping Wings	37
Memories	38
Sick Birdie	39
And Soon It's Over	41
She's Gone	43
The End	45
Acknowledgements	47
About the Author	48

Forward

When I was a little girl, growing up in the country, we always had a pet of some sort…a cat, a dog, etc. On occasion we would go to our Amish grandparents' house in Burton Station, Ohio, for a visit or a delicious meal. I have admired my grandmother my entire life and have always wanted to be like her.

Gramma Yoder enjoyed gardening, home making, cooking, baking, sewing and being out in nature. I can never think of a time that she didn't have a beautiful male yellow Canary bird, singing, perched in his cage, sitting in the dining room amongst her indoor plants. I don't recall his name, but he always sang a happy tune. I thought that someday I would like to have a bird that could sing.

Romeo

Time has a way of getting along. I grew up, married, had five wonderful children, eleven super grandchildren and nine marvelous great-grandchildren. As my husband, Glen, and I were raising our five children, we had the opportunity to obtain a "wild" African Parrot from Africa through Moore's Missionaries. We were excited about our new pet and named him *ROMEO*.

Now Romeo was not a happy camper. He certainly did not want to be held, just fed and watered. We had him about seven years when he came down with pneumonia; Romeo had been on the porch of the garage when Glen (we called him Dad), took him out of the cage and held him until he died that afternoon. It was sad; we buried him in one of the Begonia flower beds.

RIP

Bird

Several years later, my husband bought a cute little red Volkswagen diesel pickup truck. He was anxious to take it on a trip so we went on a two-week vacation to Sarasota, Florida and stayed at Sis Sollers' mother's mobile home.

The next day Dad said he wanted to go sight-seeing, so off we went. Instead, we visited several shops and malls. I didn't know it at the time, but Dad had his mind set on finding a "hand-fed" baby African Grey Parrot! Wouldn't you know, in this one particular pet shop, we see a sign in the window saying *"Hand-fed Baby African Greys."*

In a flash we went in, found a clerk and asked him about the "babies". "Oh, they are too young to be here all day," he said. "If you are really interested, I can bring them in tomorrow for you to see them."

Dad was ecstatic! I thought, "Oh my, this is turning out to be an expensive stop!" When Dad asked how much a bird cost, the clerk replied, "$1200.00." Using my math, I had it all figured out: the birds were eight weeks old and that meant that each feather and fuzz cost about a dollar each.

We selected a feisty little baby and named him "BIRD." We left and had to wait until the day we were returning to Ohio before we could pick him up.

(I must mention here that we didn't eat out or spend any money from that point on so we could pay for Bird!)

The day finally came for us to leave for Ohio, so off to the pet store we went. Sure enough, when we got to the pet shop, Bird, some baby bird food and the bill were waiting for us. The clerk put Bird in a small, cedar-lined aquarium with a screen on top. He gave us quite a few jars of frozen baby bird food, a syringe and instructions on how to feed him.

There were no guarantees on the bird whatsoever. Instructions for feeding said we should not feed the bird until his craw was empty or his food will spoil in his craw.

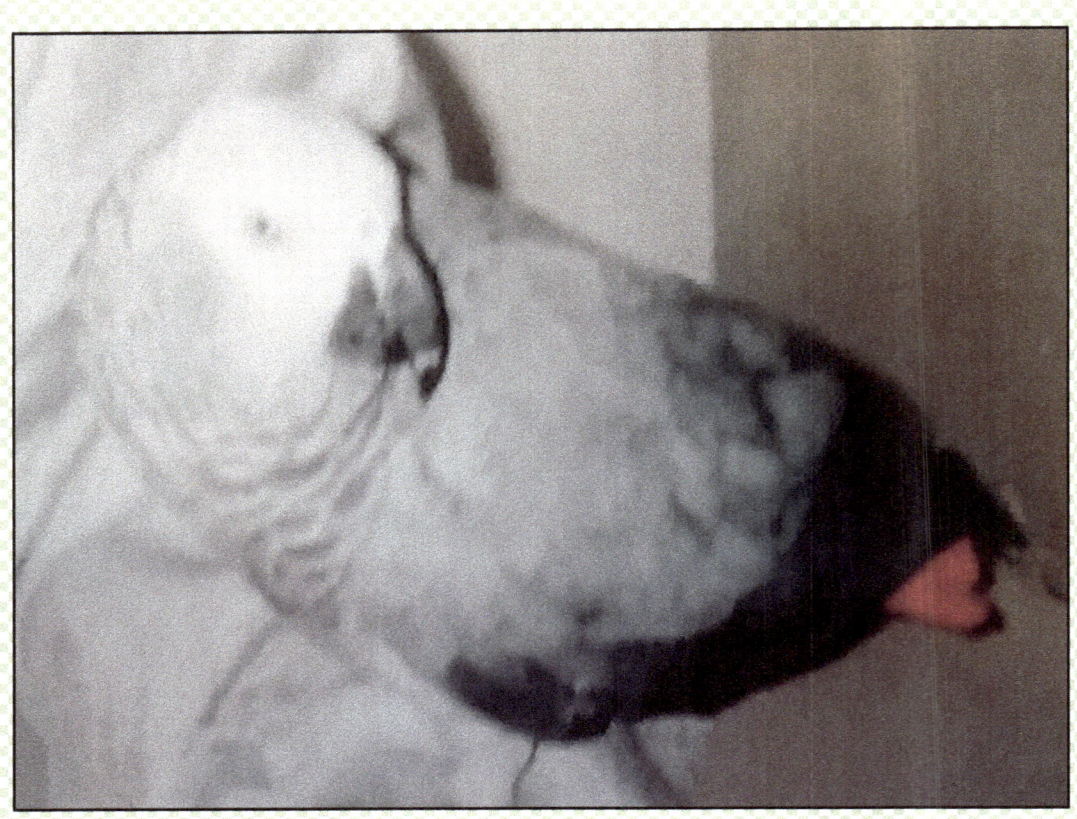

Going Home

"Well, we are finally on our way home, Bird!" I say. Now this was in January and the further north we went, the colder it became. I kept Bird in his cage on my lap throughout most of the eleven-hour trip.

Whenever it was time to feed Bird, we would stop at a road-side café or restaurant and Dad would run in to have a jar of food heated. Dad would say to the servers, "Would you heat the baby's food?" They would ask him what it was and Dad replied, "I don't know; it's for a baby bird." They all would have a good laugh.

Back on the road as I was feeding Bird, whenever a truck went by it would scare him and he would move his beak. Oh, my! I would have food all over his face.

On the way home, we stopped in Columbia, North Carolina to spend the night with one of Gramma Shevel's cousins. Everyone there loved our new baby!

All the way home I felt sorry for Bird in the aquarium, so I often put him on my shoulder under my shirt. He loved traveling that way. I didn't know at the time, but Bird was bonding with his new "Mommy." He liked that and he never once went potty on me the whole way home.

Back in Ohio

When we arrived back home in Ohio, it was ten degrees and snowy. I didn't have a snow-suit for Bird so we wrapped up the aquarium and rushed him into the house. Since we didn't know we would have a baby bird when we got home, we went directly to the pet store for supplies. Dad picked out a cage while I was busy getting toys, a T-stand and some assorted grains for when Bird was ready to eat them. We hurried back home to introduce Bird to his new home.

We put cedar chips on the bottom of the cage, the rung on the lowest setting, and water in his dish. Dad put Bird on one of the rungs. Bird held on as tight as he could, but soon he was hanging upside-down. He looked at us as if saying, "Is this what I am supposed to be doing?" We laughed so hard!

Red Tail Feathers

Feedings went well and Bird was growing bigger. The last place for feathers to grow out was on his breast. When we brought him home, you could barely see his red tail. However, within a month the feathers were almost all grown out. It was amazing to see.

Bird was now sitting on the rung in the middle of his cage. He drank water well and soon he was also eating the grains; he loved sun-flower seeds and peanuts.

By now Bird rode on my shoulder often.

Learning to Speak

Bird loved to "help" me and at an early age, when he would go potty, I taught him to say, "Bird go vvt!" I would put him back in his cage; then he would say, "go vvt" and return to my shoulder. He was potty trained just like a child.

Bird also loved to be in the kitchen with me, however, I had to keep an eye on him because he loved to chew on everything.

When Bird was about a year old, I realized he could say some words. "Hello" and "I Love You" were easy. It was Christmas time so "Merry Christmas" were his next words.

Parrots and humans learn to talk at about the same age. I wished I had spent even more time with Bird teaching him colors and shapes. He learned so easily.

Merry Christmas

One weekend Dad and I decided to go away for a couple of days. Our good neighbor, Bill, said he would love to keep Bird while we were gone. Bird was only about one year old and picked up every word spoken. "Merry Christmas" and "Praise the Lord" were his favorite phrases. Well, Bill got so tired of hearing Bird say "Praise the Lord" that he told the bird, "B*** S***, Bird." It took several years to make Bird forget those words. He would catch people unawares, and when they would hear Bird say those bad words, Bird would just repeat them again.

From then on, we left Bird at a pet shop whenever we went away. The pet shop owner told us to never leave Bird alone for any length of time; Bird wouldn't eat.

The Farm in Greenford

In 1983, my husband and I bought twenty-five acres of land in Greenford, Ohio. Sometimes we would take Bird with us to the farm while we did clean-up work. Bird always enjoyed traveling; it was amazing.

In 1986 my brother, Ellis, and his boys poured the cement for our new double-wide mobile home; a new garage addition was also added. Finally the day came that we moved out to the farm and we sold our Shields Road property. Bird, Dad and I, along with all our belongings, got settled on Lisbon Road in Greenford.

The Great Escape

One rainy morning Dad went to work and I got busy around the house. Bird was helping me, so when I went outside to bury some scraps and coffee grounds in the flower beds, Bird sat on my shoulder. When a hard wind blew, off Bird flew. He came back and almost landed on my shoulder when off again he went. He flew up into a very large tree in the woods.

I did everything I could to get him to come back, all to no avail. He was gone! I was crying, wet, wind-blown and absolutely devastated. Our little bird was out in the wild with red-tailed hawks, foxes that loved chicken, and unscrupulous weather to say the least.

I actually got on the phone and called the Highway Patrol, the Sheriff's Office, three television stations and the Canfield Police. Then it dawned on me to call my husband before he heard about it at work. His company gave Dad the rest of the day off so he could help look for Bird.

When Dad arrived home he changed his clothes and soon we were out checking every tree. "Yep, there he is!" hollered Dad. Bird still would not come down; he was enjoying his freedom too much. By then the weather had cleared up some so my husband suggested we set his cage out in the open with Bird's favorite nuts and seeds. "Perhaps he will come down and go in the coop," he said.

Late afternoon came and still no sight of that bundle of grey feathers with a red tail. Bird was gone! Dad said, "Let's get on our bikes and ride all the back roads." Let me tell you, those back roads are mostly hills, not level at all. By dark we were exhausted, but we wouldn't give up. We wrote a brief description of Bird and gave copies to about thirty of our neighbors.

The next day all dispatchers not scheduled to work came out to help look for Bird. We walked through the woods and fields, all to no avail. I remember a friend named Tom came with his large fishing net, hoping to catch our little bird; not a word, sound or glimpse of Bird all day.

The next day, while Dad was at work, I again drove every road and talked to everyone I could find, hoping to find Bird. There was no news anywhere. Bird may be lost forever. I asked God for help in finding Bird safe and sound or to find his body so we would have the satisfaction knowing what happened.

When my husband got home on the third evening of Bird's absence, I fixed dinner, but neither of us was hungry. We missed Bird and just had to find him. We left the table and were about to leave to go looking again when the phone rang. It was our friend at the Canfield Police Station. He said that someone had called from Dreamy Acres Farm over on Route 46. They told him they had seen a grey bird with a red tail in a pine tree. Boys were throwing him popcorn.

I yelled to Glen that Bird has been spotted. Quickly he put the cage in the back of the truck and off we went. When we got there, as we drove down a long driveway, we could see Bird in a tree. Bird knew the truck, so when Bird saw us getting out of the truck, he flew right to us, landed on my shoulder and gave me a big kiss. He was so glad to see us! We both hugged Bird; he wasn't about to fly off my shoulder again. We brought him home and put him in his cage. When we locked the door, Bird said, "Whew!".

We offered a reward to the people that found Bird and everyone was happy at the end of this long ordeal. We were glad to have this ordeal over with.

Sweet Memories

My husband always called me "Tweet" and I called him "Honey." Little ears picked up on that and at times I didn't know if Dad was calling me or if it was Bird. Bird also called Dad "Honey" at times. Bird also learned to give kisses. Sweet memories!

Bird always ate breakfast with Dad. He loved to tease Bird and Bird learned to retaliate a bit too aggressively. Never the less, they both loved to play Bird games.

Sometimes my husband would get nipped and wonder why. One day when Dad was shaving, Bird flew into the bathroom and bit right through his ear; Bird didn't want that razor touching Dad's face. Strange!

Here We Go A-Traveling

We had a motorhome for a few years and belonged to the Good Sam Camping Club. Bird always went with us and was always the center of attraction. We would put him outside immediately after arriving at our destination. Bird learned to whistle at the women walking by. One day we, and several other couples, decided to go sight-seeing. The other campers, that stayed behind, offered to watch Bird as he sat in the shade. After a while, a little old lady, dressed as a worn-out "Barbie Doll," walked by. Bird kept giving her the wolf-whistle and she kept looking around to see who it was. We know, don't we!

Bird always knew when we were getting ready to travel. Whenever he saw suitcases in the hall or the motorhome in the driveway, he would say," Bird go bye-bye," or "Bird go camper."

His cage was fastened directly behind my seat so he had a good view out the window. When we turned a corner, he would sway, holding on to his perch and say, "Hold on, Bird!"

Off to Alaska

In the year 2001 we, along with twenty-two other Good Sam campers, went on a drive to Alaska. What an awesome trip that was. Of course, Bird was packed and on his way to Alaska with us.

Prior to leaving, we drove to Niagara Falls to check with Customs to see what was needed to take Bird into Canada and back. The woman at Customs told us we wouldn't need anything for one bird. Wrong!

We left Ohio and drove through North Dakota to the Canadian Border. Going through Customs, we had Bird's Bill of Sale which described him and his identity. When asked for his *Cites Permit*, we told the agent what we had been told at the Niagara Falls Customs Office; we didn't need any special papers. This was wrong. An exotic bird requires a *Cites Permit*. We were told we could get one at the Fish and Wildlife Game Office in Skagway.

After a half hour delay, the agent told us that when we get up to Skagway we must immediately go to the Fish and Wildlife Game Office and "legalize" Bird. Meanwhile, between Canada and Alaska is the Yukon Territory. Since it belongs to the United States, we had to repeat the whole procedure again explaining our error. Once we reached Skagway, we immediately went to the Fish and Wildlife Game Office. We finally were given the proper papers to show every time we crossed a border.

Bird was a great traveler and we had a wonderful time in Alaska.

On our return trip we were re-entering the United States through Montana. Oh my, the Border Agent there was not pleasant to us at all. He told us that we, Bird and the motorhome were not going anywhere. The young Ranger gave us a hard time for over an hour and refused to call Skagway to clear Bird. I told my husband to keep his cool; don't say or do anything. We thought the

Ranger wanted to keep Bird. I told Glen they would never do such a thing; then I left and headed for the motorhome.

As the Ranger came toward the motorhome to see Bird, I went in and told Bird, "Daddy and Mommy are in deep trouble and we have to pray right now." Bird looked at me as if to say, "But it's not my bedtime yet." We prayed and then I went outside again.

Right then it so happened that it was shift change. A much older Ranger joined us and we explained the whole situation again to him. Within 15 minutes we were back on the road again. When we arrived back home, we soon obtained a *Cites Permit* and sent a copy to the Border Patrol. We got the nicest note in return. "Whew!"

Bird's Talents

When Bird was about three years old, my mom and Grandpa John were delighted that Bird could whistle. Grandpa taught Bird the song *"Bridge Over the River Kwai."* Bird whistled every note.

And Bird often tried to answer the phone. When it rang, Bird would say, "Greenford farm, yes, okay, well, bye-bye." When the doorbell would ring, he would answer, "Come in."

One day the UPS man delivered a package at our front door. Bird was inside and said loudly, "Come in." About that time my husband came around the house just as the UPS man was coming out the door. Embarrassed, he told Glen that he was sorry, but someone had told him to come in and when he did, only a bird was there. Bird had spoken in Glen's voice.

Leaving the Farm

When we had cats, Bird always knew their names. Whenever we left the house, I would always call, "Penny Jo, PV!" so I could put them outdoors. Bird would help too. He would say, "Where is Penny Jo? Where is PV?", etc.

In 1996 we sold the farm and bought a place in Florida. We left Bosch, our black lab, at the farm, her favorite stomping ground; Bird came with us.

Bird enjoyed Florida. Whenever we would go somewhere without the motorhome, one of our friends would keep Bird for us. Bird would sulk and not make friends for a day or so, just to let them know he was sad that we had left him behind.

An Egg?

One day we left Bird with our friend, Jan. We said our goodbyes to Bird and left. About a half-hour later we received a call from her. She asked me if Bird had laid any eggs before. I replied, "No! He's a male."

"Well, he just laid one," Jan said. We rushed back over to Jan's to congratulate Bird and declare officially that she was our *little girl*. Oh, how she loved that. She hadn't been the same since. We decided to call her *BIRDIE*!

Birdie

Now we understood why Bird liked to be in the kitchen with me so much; she is a girl and loves the kitchen. Birdie often played in a paper bag on the left side of the sink. She knew her boundaries, but sometimes she would nibble on my cookbook. I would say to her, "No, no," and then she would respond, "Bad Bird." Of course, *Birdie* loved her new name.

Birdie had her own room where she had an excellent view of the back yard. At a given command, Birdie would fly from her room to the kitchen to give me a kiss. We also often put her cage on the back porch where she could interact with various neighbors.

One time my husband was sleeping on the couch when Birdie climbed off her cage onto the floor and then onto the couch where Glen was sleeping. She just sat there watching him. She loved her "Daddy," on her terms.

Birdie loved people food, but of course no chocolate or onions. She loved ice cream and never dropped a speck. Chicken leg bones were her favorite; she would split the bones and eat the marrow, very good for her. Birdie would often hold a potato chip in her claw and never break it. If I tried to take a chip from her, forget it! She was very possessive of her treats.

Bed Time

Every night, when I would put Birdie in her cage and tuck her in bed, I would pray, "Now I lay me down to sleep, Birdie go to sleep, Birdie go to sleep. Amen." With as many times as I prayed with her, I never heard her pray out loud.

One night we were visiting at my daughter, Glenda's home when my husband decided to call it a night; he would go to bed and would take Birdie with him. He hopped into bed, turned off the light and said good night to Birdie. About ten minutes later, in the darkness, he heard, "Now I me."

Glen called me into the room and told me what the bird had said. Birdie wanted to say her prayers so she could go to sleep.

If we stayed up late and Birdie was tired, she would say, "Bird go sleep."

Another Egg?

It was back in 2006 when I noticed that Birdie was not acting right. She would eat and then make hurtful little noises that meant she was in pain. I then realized she was trying to lay another egg.

My husband and I took her to a well-known Bird Vet in Winter Haven to have her checked out. The Vet said she was a very sick little bird; he gave us a couple of options. The first option was that we could leave Birdie at the Vet for three days at a cost of $300.00. Then, if he had to remove the egg surgically, hoping it didn't break, it would cost more. The other option was that he would give Birdie a shot of calcium; we then would take her home and soak her in very warm water for five minutes every day. We chose the second option.

Well, if you know me, you know that I don't give up very easily. I told Birdie that her doctor wants her to bathe in warm water and that is just what we were going to do. I explained to her that she had to lay that egg. That was on a Friday and I faithfully bathed her, not once, but three times a day. This was a miracle; birds do not like to be soaked. While she was soaking, I would sing *"Jesus Loves Me."* She truly did trust her mommy. Then it would take another two hours to get her dry using a very warm towel.

On Tuesday morning I checked her and told my husband, "Birdie is going to lay that egg!" I put her back on the roost in her cage and in about two minutes out flew the egg. Birdie was so excited. It then took her all afternoon to clean out her system. She was plugged up since the egg was in the way.

We celebrated with her and thanked Jesus for giving Birdie back to us.

The Old Birdie

Birdie copied peoples' laughs and welcomed guests as they came to the door. She rang her bell when she wanted attention, or better yet, she would say, "Out."

She would copy people's laughter, sneezes, or clearing throats. She would bark like a dog or quack just like a duck when she heard the ducks on the lake.

I would use a spray bottle of water when she needed correction and Birdie would tell me, "Go on!"

Her favorite foods were chicken leg marrow, hot dogs, coffee, cereal, milk, ice cream and hamburgers.

We would tell Birdie whenever we were going bird shopping. When we arrived back home, we would let her open the bags to see her food and a new toy.

Clipping Wings

When we went North for the summer, we would stop at The Pet Shop in Boardman and have her wings clipped. Birdie loved to go in that shop because Mickey was kind to her and there were so many toys she could look at.

When we got to daughter Ruthie's home, Birdie would try to fly; she would land on the floor, kerplunk.

Our son, David, had a beautiful birdcage for us to use while we were at Ruthie's; her traveling cage was small and Birdie needed a big playhouse.

Memories

We have so many memories of Birdie. Her life touched so many other family members, friends and neighbors over the years. Birdie was a female, yet could talk like Glen. Our girls would tease me and say "Mom, we don't know about that Birdie!"

Sick Birdie

In April 2009, we packed our Honda Odyssey van, with Birdie of course, and headed for Ohio to attend the Johnston Alumni Banquet and the Yoder reunion in Middlefield. In route we stopped in Virginia to visit our friends, Ron and Dee. They had rented a place in the Hollers for the summer; it was beautiful there.

While visiting, Birdie was able to have her cage right in front of the picture window overlooking the front porch. Here Birdie could keep her eye on everything and everyone.

I had noticed a watery red in her stool and mentioned it to my husband. He thought Birdie had been eating a lot of strawberries. We left early Monday morning so we could arrive at Ruthie's by five o'clock that evening. Birdie ate lightly while traveling, yet she still said some words.

We got settled in at Ruthie's and noticed that Birdie was quiet. She would pick and choose her food though she did drink water. In the evening I would rock her and sing to her; she loved it. She would actually fall asleep like that.

Thursday morning, I informed my husband that Birdie had been passing blood clots and that she needed to see Dr. Allen, a very good bird doctor. We left early and were there by 9 a.m.

Dr. Allen very lovingly took Birdie and checked her mouth. She was okay there. After further examination, he checked Birdie's stool and informed us that she had cancer. We couldn't believe it.

He gave her a shot and told us that within two hours we would know which way she would go. We both felt that the difficulty she had laying her second egg may have caused the cancer.

Ruthie took Dad to his doctor appointment and then came back to stay with Birdie and me. She then left again to pick him up and bring him back to Dr. Allen's. They both came in and asked how Birdie was. I was crying so hard because, by then, I knew I was going to lose Birdie.

With heavy hearts, we put Birdie into her *kitty carrier* while we returned to Ruthie's. I held Birdie and rocked her almost the entire afternoon. She snuggled on my chest under my chin. That evening we had to go to Linda and David's for about two hours; we left Birdie at home. When we got home, I went to Birdie's cage and reached for her to come to me. She just sat there; I had to pry her off her roost. Yes, I knew that the end was near.

And Soon it was Over

I hurried into the bedroom and put on my jammies. I told my husband, who was already in bed, that I was going to hold Birdie through the night. I put a towel over my chest and placed Birdie right over my heart. She could hear every beat as we went to bed. We said our prayers, "Now I lay me down to sleep, Birdie go to sleep. Yes, Birdie, you can go to sleep, it's okay."

I sang ever so softly and right after midnight I realized she was gone. Very carefully, I got up, wrapped her in the towel and placed her in a safe spot. Then I went to bed and cried myself to sleep. It was June 11, 2009. She was 25 ½ years old while the average lifespan is typically 70 to 75 years.

She's Gone

When morning came, I notified my family that Birdie was gone. We all were sad as we got dressed. Ruthie advised us that David had dug Birdie's grave and that we could have a proper burial.

I had some silver wrapping paper with stars on it. I wrapped Birdie in a soft paper towel and then in the wrapping paper. We went to David's house; his flower garden was beautiful in the back yard. It is here that I laid Birdie in her final resting place.

The End

What a wonderful adventure we all had with Birdie. I am sure there will be at least one African Grey Parrot with a red tail in heaven, flying all around.

Those beautiful flowers are still there. I thank God so often that He allowed me to have such a fine pet as Birdie. I was able to give her love, and in so many ways she was able to give love back.

Birdie

Acknowledgements

I want to thank my children, Glenda, Debra, David, Tim and Ruthie, who may have thought they took second place to this beloved bird.

I would like to thank my daughter, Ruthie, for encouraging me to record my memories of Birdie, and then to have this book published.

A special thank you to my son, David. He was kind enough to bury my feathered friend and continue to maintain Birdie's grave to this day.

The cover drawing of Birdie was made by my very talented granddaughter, Kate. Thank you so much.

And I will always be grateful to my late husband, Glen, for bringing Birdie into my life.

About the Author

Helen Yoder and Glen Shevel were married on July 24, 1953 and over the years lived in Ohio and Florida. After Glen passed away, Helen moved to Tennessee where, as a widow, she now resides in Hendersonville, Tennessee. They are the parents of five children, eleven grandchildren and seventeen great-grandchildren.

Like her Amish grandmother, Helen's passions include baking, cooking, sewing and gardening. In 2019 she authored a cookbook, *"Helen's Kitchen Cookbook Favorites,"* published by Baird Farms Publishing Company LLC.

"Life with Birdie, The African Grey Parrot," is based on memories and notes recorded over the years that Birdie lived with Helen and Glen.

www.ingramcontent.com/pod-product-compliance
Lightning Source LLC
Chambersburg PA
CBHW041220240426
43661CB00012B/1095